Shade of Love

Luz Torres-Sepe

Illustrated by Page Publishing

PAGE PUBLISHING
Conneaut Lake, PA

First originally published by Page Publishing 2022

ISBN 978-1-6624-7123-0 (pbk)
ISBN 978-1-6624-7125-4 (digital)

Printed in the United States of America

To my husband, Robert, and our children—Robbie, Crissy, and
Emi Sepe—for all your love and support through the years!

To Jose M. Mendez for being an example of
what hope looks like—to never give up!

To all the children of the world!

How good is your loving mercy O'God! The children
of men take cover under the shade of your wings.
—Psalm 36:7

Paint with love,
a shade of love.

A covenant filled with God's shade.
The color green, the color blue.

The kind that always remains.
The color red "bringing life," he says.

And coat after coat he applies.
All through my life all the time.

And then spreads the white just in time.
In holiness, his holiness.

He said to color, with a shade of love.
He said to honor with a shade of love.

Paint with love.
A shade of love.

For all of the days, which seem gloom.
A heavenly blue, bringing good news!

And all of the days that seem hard.
Purple, yellow, my Jesus fellow!

The shade that was given to me.
It's filled with love streams.
Jesus loves streams.

And gives me a crown with the brown.
And pearls of black, we became a pack!

So let's go color with a shade of love.
So let's go honor with a shade of love.

Paint with love, a shade of love.

What do you think a shade of love is?
(Color your shade of love.)

Answer: How good and pleasant it is when
brothers live together in unity (Psalm 133:1).

A covenant filled with God's shade.
The color green, the color blue.

The kind that always remains.
The color red "bringing life," he says.

Above all, clothe yourselves with love, which binds
us all together in perfect harmony. (Colossians 3:14)

About the Author

Dedos Photography

Luz Torres-Sepe is an early-childhood teacher. Happily married, she is a mother of three. Also, she is a worship leader, singer, and songwriter.